Introduction

The world will see the Arctic Ocean rise as a strategically important maritime commons in the mid to late 21st century. Sea-ice has historically been the barrier to development and economic activity in the Arctic Ocean littorals. That condition is changing as the coastal areas of the North American and Eurasian continents are seeing longer periods of reduced ice coverage during the annual June to October summer thaw.[1] Reduced sea-ice will create two favorable conditions for Arctic development and economic activity, navigable shipping lanes through the Arctic Ocean open and petroleum resources become accessible and exploitable. World interest in the Arctic will increase as economic activity in the Arctic becomes more viable due to the reduced ice coverage.

Increased worldwide attention on the Arctic affects the United States and the pursuit of its Arctic interests. The United States recognizes the potential in the Arctic for economic gain and the potential for a greater military presence in the region.[2] The Naval Services will see an increased requirement to operate in the Arctic, protecting US sovereignty by providing maritime security and ensuring free-passage through international waters. This paper investigates the Marine Corps role in the Arctic Ocean littorals in the context of the Single Naval Battle concept and the Marine Air Ground Task Force (MAGTF).

Marine Corps long-range planning, beyond 2025, must account for a strategically important Arctic Ocean and begin developing concepts for the employment of amphibious forces in an Arctic littoral environment. The unique Arctic environment brings the potential for new operational concepts and non-traditional uses and configurations of the MAGTF. An Arctic MAGTF will function differently than a western Pacific MAGTF or a Mediterranean MAGTF by performing different missions and requiring different capabilities.

Under the Single Naval Battle concept, a MAGTF uniquely fills the sea control capability gaps the Navy faces in the Arctic. A properly equipped MAGTF could establish multi-domain control of the straits and approaches to the Arctic Ocean to deny or ensure access to resources and movement through the Arctic shipping lanes. Sea control is only one example of a potential Arctic MAGTF mission, but one that raises interesting force structure and capability implications for the Marine Corps.

This paper attempts to accomplish four objectives to illustrate the need to develop concepts like an Arctic MAGTF in a sea-control mission. The first is to capture a sense of the future long-term strategic importance of the Arctic by describing the changing environment and framing the Arctic security problem in the context of the global implications of those changes. The second point describes the current national and DoD strategic level policy on the Arctic and highlights potential changes to those policies that will cue Marine Corps planners that the design of an Arctic operational concept should begin. The third objective is to illustrate to the Marine Corps the necessity of considering Arctic littoral operations in its long-term planning. Lastly, this paper addresses the operational limitations the joint force faces in the Arctic to frame future Marine Corps capability development.

This paper does not advocate for an immediate change to current policies and plans. The issues and considerations presented will likely rise to prominence in the 2025-2050 timeframe, outside of the planning window described in current Marine Corps strategic documents. As such, this research serves to inform the current Marine Corps planners and capability developers researching the Arctic and intends to spark a discussion on the future Arctic within the Marine Corps.

There is a large degree of uncertainty about the future Arctic. Predicting when and how the environment will change is difficult. Discussing the Arctic and future military operations in that region beyond 2025 requires an assumption that the current trends in Arctic ice melt will continue, enabling greater shipping traffic and resource exploitation. One must also assume that the shipping traffic and resource exploitation activity in the Arctic will become significant enough to warrant a military presence in the Arctic that is greater than the present day. A final assumption is that the future National Security Strategy and corresponding National Military Strategy will demand a greater military presence in the Arctic.

The Operational Environment

Designing an operation in the Arctic begins with framing the Arctic environment. The Arctic Ocean is an ice-covered ocean bounded by the continental landmasses of North America and Eurasia. Three accepted definitions describe the geographic boundaries of the Arctic. Countries, governments, and non-government organizations may utilize any of the three when referring to the region, complicating a discussion on the Arctic. The common geographic definitions of the Arctic are: the area north of the limit of upright tree growth on the North American and Eurasian continents, high latitude locations where the average daily summer temperature does not rise above 10 degrees Celsius and the Arctic Circle, or the circular area south of the north pole where the sun does not set between 21 June (the summer solstice) and 21 December (the winter solstice).[3] The Arctic Circle defines the Arctic region for the purpose of this paper. (See Figure 1 for a graphic depiction of the three Arctic definitions.)

The region within the Arctic Circle comprises 6 percent of the earth's surface, or approximately 8,100,000 square miles.[4] Ice covers the Arctic Ocean for the majority of the year and only submarines or ice-capable and icebreaking ships can access the ocean. Ice formation in the Arctic is cyclical. During the warmer summer months of July through October the sea-ice thins and recedes. Over the winter months the ice thickens and re-freezes. The ice conditions in the Arctic, however, are changing.

The Arctic ice cap, or Polar ice cap, which limits sea surface navigation, is shrinking. Yearly ice cover in the Arctic has lost 10 percent of its size every decade since the 1970's.[5] The sea-ice loss is accelerating and the littoral areas of the Arctic Ocean are experiencing summer periods (July to October) with no ice cover present. Climate and ice flow models indicate the Arctic littoral regions may see ice coverage free summer periods by 2037.[6]

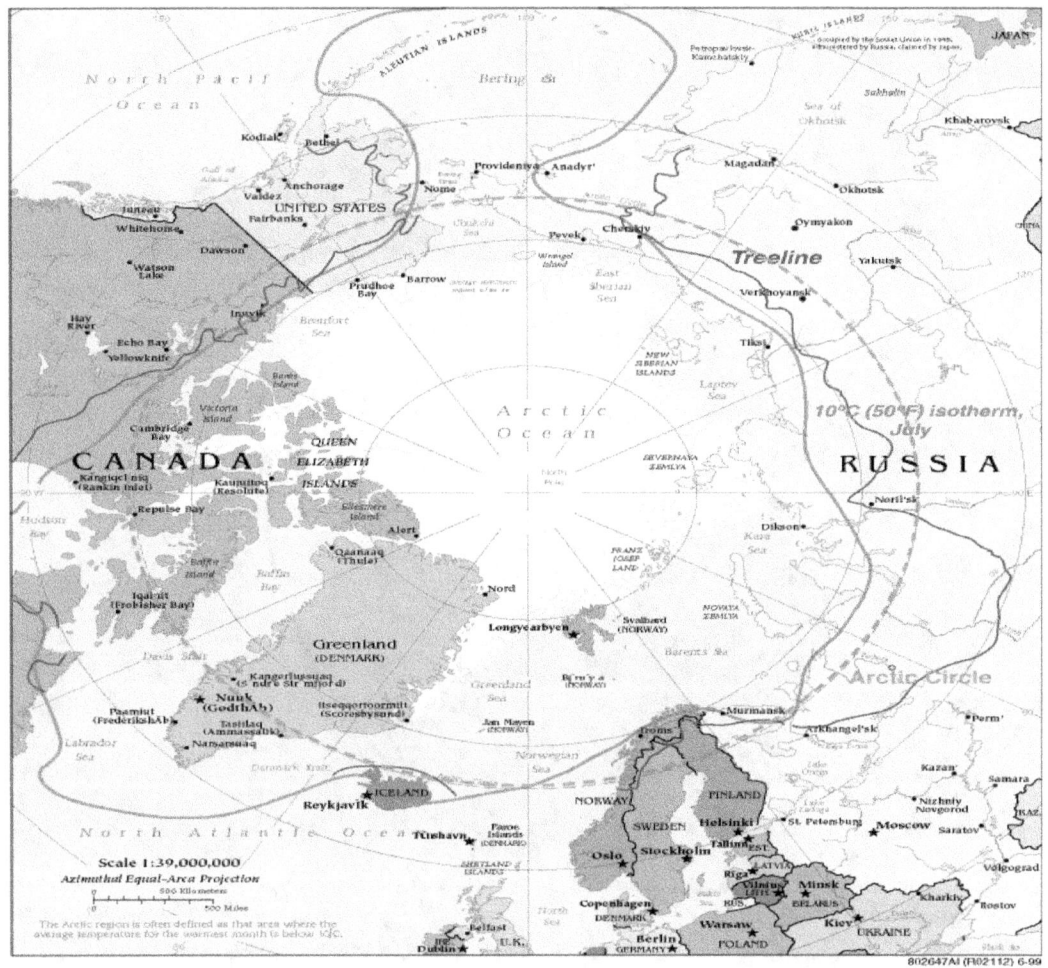

Figure 1: The Arctic Region Boundaries. (From: The US National Snow and Ice Data Center)[7]

Two sea routes are open in the Arctic Ocean littorals during the ice-free periods (see figure 2). The Northern Sea Route (NSR) extends along the Arctic coast of Russia from the Barents Sea to the Bering Strait. The Northwest Sea Route, or Northwest Passage (NWP), transits US waters and the Canadian Arctic Archipelago from the Bering Strait to the Davis Strait.[8] Since 2007, the NSR and the NWP have been ice-cover free and open to shipping during the summer months.

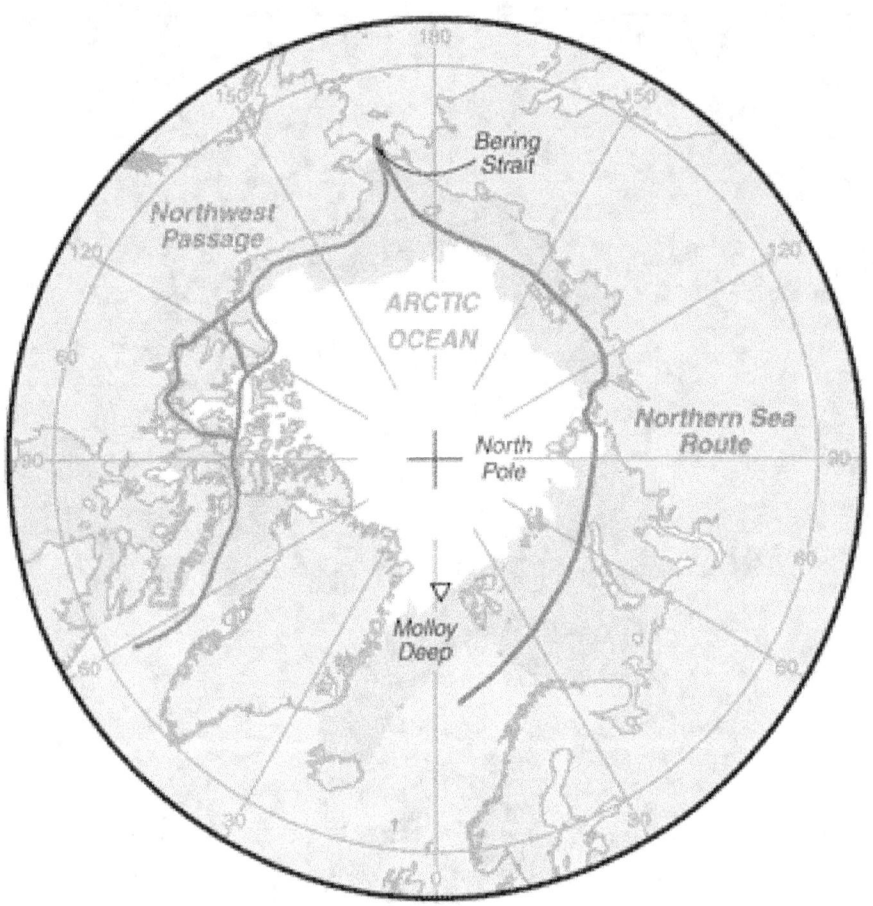

Figure 2: Map of Arctic Sea Route (From: CIA World Factbook) [9]

The Arctic Ocean joins the Atlantic and Pacific Oceans through a series of narrow waterways and straits. These natural chokepoints provide ships and submarines access to the NWP and the NSR. The most notable strait, and natural chokepoint in U.S territory, is the Bering Strait between Alaska and Russia. The Bering Strait is 85 kilometers wide at its narrowest point, and the NWP and NSR access the Pacific Ocean by transiting the Chukchi Sea through the Bering Strait to the Bering Sea in the south.

The NWP transits the Canadian Arctic Archipelago, which is a large area of islands and mainland coast with 36,000 individual pieces of dry land above sea level. [10] Five primary routes through the Archipelago make up the NWP; each route is viable, depending on the ice conditions and the size of the ship making the transit. [11] Numerous straits and narrows constrain the NWP routes throughout their length. On the western side of the NWP the routes pass through the Amundsen Gulf, which is 90 km wide at its narrowest, or the M'Clure Strait, which is 120 km wide at its narrowest. On the eastern end of the NWP, the routes transit either the Hudson Strait at 100 km wide or the Lancaster Sound at 80 km wide to enter the Davis Strait between Canada and Greenland.

The NSR is similar to the NWP in that a vessel may transit several routes depending on ice conditions and vessel characteristics. Five seas comprise the NSR, the Barents, Kara, Laptev, East Siberian and Chukchi.[12] Restrictive straits link the five seas, which serve as chokepoints to cut the NSR. The navigable straits between the Barents, Kara, Laptev and East Siberian seas range from 53 km to 57 km wide. The Long Strait between the East Siberian and Chukchi Sea is 139 km wide.[13]

Straits and narrow waterways are militarily significant geographic characteristics of the NWP and the NSR. These natural chokepoints offer a military force control of surface ship traffic through the Arctic passages. Defending these straits and keeping the passages open will be important to any country that relies on the Arctic for resources or mobility.

Global and US Interest in the Arctic

The Arctic sea routes present opportunities to the global shipping interests. Routing ships through the Arctic nearly halves the shipping distance between Europe and Asia, compared to routing ships through the Suez or Panama Canals.[14] Travelling via the NSR reduces the shipping time from Yokohama, Japan, to Hamburg, Germany, by 11 days as compared to the Suez Canal. Ships average approximately a 20 percent savings in fuel as well. Total savings for one large petroleum tanker ship in fuel costs and canal fees are approximately $200,800 in 2012 fuel prices.[15]

Interest in the Arctic routes and use of the Arctic routes is growing and traffic is increasing on the NSR in particular. From 2007 to 2010, 21 ships transited the NSR. Forty-one ships transited in 2011: 26 cargo ships and 14 non-cargo ships. In 2012, 46 total ships, 35 cargo ships and 11 other non-cargo ships, transited the NSR carrying 1,022,577 tons of cargo.[16] Using the cost savings figures above and assuming that the savings for each ship are relatively the same, the shipping industry saved $7,028,000 on the NSR. The economic benefit of shortened shipping distances is an attractive proposition that will bring greater shipping activity as the ice continues to diminish and access to the Arctic passages increases.

The NSR is becoming a global energy transportation route. Of note in the NSR transportation figures above, 22 of the 62 cargo-carrying ships transported natural gas and petroleum products from Europe and Russia to China, South Korea, and Thailand.[17] If this trend continues, then a shift in the patterns of global energy shipping is beginning and the strategic importance of the NSR will rise.

The NWP, the sea route over North America, is not as active as the NSR. Very little cargo shipping transits the NWP. In 2010 and 2011 the majority of the shipping traffic was research ships and tourist cruise ships.[18] There are fewer less ports, less infrastructure and fewer icebreakers in the NWP than the NSR to support shipping. Canada is considering increasing the capability of the NWP to support commercial shipping by upgrading several of its northern ports. The NWP is likely to experience more traffic in the future as shipping above North America becomes more viable and Canada increases its support infrastructure.

The shrinking sea-ice is not only opening new shipping routes but it is also opening access to natural resources. Arctic oil is abundant and strategically valuable to all of the Arctic countries. Approximately 10 percent of the world's known petroleum reserves and a projected 25-40 percent of world wide undiscovered reserves lie in the Arctic.[19] These estimates are based on conventional oil and gas sources and do not include oil shale and methane gas hydrates.[20] Newer extraction methods and sources could significantly increase the available petroleum in the Arctic Ocean. There is not yet enough data collected from Arctic exploration to estimate these other sources.[21].

The Arctic oil and gas resources available to the United States are valuable. The US Arctic economic exclusion zone (EEZ) contains 30 billion barrels of estimated oil reserves and 221 trillion cubic feet of natural gas.[22] At 2012 annual oil consumption rates of 7 billion barrels, the oil held in the US Arctic can supply the country for about 4 years and the natural gas can supply the country for 9 years.[23] The US Arctic is a petroleum rich region with considerable strategic value.

Canada, Norway, Denmark and Russia have significant Arctic resources of their own. Canada holds a potential 9.7 billion barrels of oil within its EEZ.[24] Russian Arctic territorial claims, disputed by Canada, Norway and the US, potentially contain 60 percent of the oil and gas resources available in the Arctic.[25] Russia is accessing more of its Arctic oil and gas reserves than any other Arctic country. It maintains a well-developed oil and gas exploitation infrastructure.[26]

The Arctic also contains mineral and fisheries resources that are potentially valuable to the Arctic countries. Manganese, copper, cobalt, zinc and gold are abundant in the Arctic.[27] These minerals lie on both the ocean floor and on the land areas within the Arctic Circle.

Warming ocean water is causing fisheries to shift north as well. Fish populations usually found in the northern Pacific and northern Atlantic oceans are moving into Arctic waters as they warm.[28] Commercial fishing fleets are following these populations.

The human population in the Arctic littorals is small, significantly smaller less than other littoral areas of the world that are generally characterized by large urban populations. Approximately 4 million people live in the Arctic region.[29] Russia holds the majority of the Arctic population with its largest city, Murmansk, maintaining a population of 307,000.[30] In comparison, the largest US population center above the Arctic Circle is Barrow, Alaska, with 4,429 residents. [31] This small Arctic population may possibly grow as activity increases, certainly as resource exploitation means become more economically viable.

The United States, Canada, Denmark, Norway and Russia bound the Arctic Ocean and make up the Arctic Five countries. Alaska provides the United States its access to the Arctic. Canada possesses a large archipelago north of its contiguous coastline in the Arctic Ocean. Denmark administers the island of Greenland to access the Arctic and Norway accesses the arctic through Svalbard Island. Russia is the largest of the Arctic Five, two thirds of the total Russian coastline is on the Arctic Ocean.[32]

Competing claims of sovereignty between the Arctic nations exist, issues that were not a priority of diplomatic effort when sea-ice limited access to the Arctic. The boundary between the United States and Canada in the Beaufort Sea remains unresolved.[33] The Russian and United States boundary agreement for the Bering Strait is still awaiting ratification by Russia.[34] Canada and Russia have competing claims on the Lomonosov Ridge that extends under the North Pole and could double the size of those countries' Arctic under-sea territory.[35] As access to the Arctic increases, resolving these competing claims will become a more urgent issue in political relations.

These competing and unresolved sovereignty claims are the greatest potential driver of increased military operations in the Arctic. Diplomacy has solved previous territorial disputes so there is no reason to doubt that the Arctic countries cannot resolve their issues peacefully.[36] It is possible, however, to generate scenarios where the nexus of high energy demands and open access to the Arctic comes together to escalate tensions in the region. Other scenarios can be drawn up that see the Arctic passages denied to countries involved in conflict outside of the Arctic. This scenario could lead to military operations aimed at opening the passages. Militarization of the Arctic is not inevitable but it is certainly plausible.

An accessible Arctic may create political and economic impacts outside of the Arctic region. A change in global shipping lanes may be occurring with petroleum products shipped through the NSR. The world may see a shift in sea-borne trade and commerce that could change the global importance of major ports and coastal cities. Current ports like Singapore, a major global shipping hub, could decline in significance while other port cities gain. Norway and Iceland are exploring developing ports to serve as Arctic shipping hubs.[37] These changes may shift the strategic calculus of the United States and possibly the emphasis the Marine Corps places on particular global regions. The history of the development of Singapore and San Francisco offer an example of the influence global shipping has on ports.

The rise of Singapore as a global shipping center is illustrative of the changes that global trade can generate. Singapore's location at the entrance to the Malacca Straits and passage between the Indian Ocean and China Sea together with its large natural harbor made it an ideal port.[38] The opening of the Suez Canal in 1869 increased traffic through Singapore by giving

European steamships a shorter route to Asia through the Red Sea, Indian Ocean, through the Malacca Straits to the western Pacific region.[39] Throughout the 19th and 20th centuries, Singapore became a chief port of call and a significant global trade hub.[40]

The modern port of Singapore is ranked number two in the world for total shipping volume, and the state of Singapore is ranked 5th in the world in gross domestic product per capita.[41] This shipping volume, and the economic prosperity it brings, could change if shipping companies decide the Arctic sea routes are more cost effective to move goods from Europe to Asia. A reduction in shipping volume through Singapore will impact Singapore's economic and political power.

San Francisco illustrates the fall of a major port city caused by changes in global shipping patterns. San Francisco grew as a major city because it was the first shipping port on the West Coast of the United States and the terminus of the transcontinental railroad.[42] In the 19th and early 20th centuries, the city was the primary port for the export and import of goods from Asia. San Francisco's economy boomed as a major port city.

Global shipping patterns changed in the latter part of the 20th century. The city of Seattle became a preferred west coast port. Seattle is one day closer to Asia than San Francisco is, US railroads were connected to that city soon after the transcontinental railroad was completed.[43] Seattle's rise created San Francisco's decline. San Francisco's economy now is primarily based on tourism and technology development, although its port facilities still receive significant business.[44]

Singapore and San Francisco are two examples of the influence global shipping routes have on port cities and the economy. The opening of the Arctic shipping routes and the potential they have in the future to change global shipping patterns could bring global changes. Cities and ports near the Arctic passages could grow in significance due to shipping, following the Singapore example. Significant cities in other parts of the world could see a decline in shipping activity and a loss of economic activity, similar to San Francisco.

The factors of increasingly viable shipping routes, strategically valuable petroleum resources, growing human population, unresolved sovereignty issues and shifting global shipping patterns add up to an increased security problem in the Arctic. Adversaries in future conflicts could see the Arctic as a strategically vital area to control, either defending their interests or attacking each other's interests. The US will be drawn to the Arctic as a country with significant interests in an open and exploitable Arctic. The US Navy and the Marine Corps face a future where they will be required to protect and advance US Arctic interests. Current US policy on the Arctic, however, does not yet fully reflect this future.

The Arctic in DOD and Marine Corps Thinking

The National Security Strategy and major DoD strategy and concept documents see the Arctic as an area of concern, but not necessarily a priority mission area for the immediate future. National policy towards the Arctic was established in 1999 with National Security Presidential Directive 66/Homeland Security Presidential Directive 25 (NSPD 66/HSPD 25), *Arctic Region Policy*. The 2010 National Security Strategy restates the broad goals of NSPD 66/HSPD 25; "The United States is an Arctic Nation with broad and fundamental interests in the Arctic region, where we seek to meet our national security needs, protect the environment, responsibly manage resources, account for indigenous communities, support scientific research, and strengthen international cooperation on a wide range of issues."[45] This twelve-year-old national policy guidance is indicative of the effort the Joint Forces should put towards preparing for the Arctic.

Updated national policy on the Arctic, when it is produced, should spur greater effort from the Marine Corps

Within the DoD the thinking on the Arctic is more robust. The 2010 Quadrennial Defense Review (QDR), which sets the four-year priorities for the DoD, generally describes the Arctic as an area of interest over the long term. The Arctic, as described in the QDR, requires close collaboration with interagency and international partners to improve human and environmental security in the region. [46] DoD will partner with the Department of State, DHS, the National Science Foundation (NSF) among others, and countries such as Russia, Canada and Norway to operate in the Arctic.

The 2011 National Military Strategy describes the Arctic only as creating a need to partner with Canada to address the security issues in that "evolving" region.[47] The 2012 Defense Strategic Guidance (DSG), which describes a rebalancing to the Asia-Pacific region, makes no mention of the Arctic as focus area for the US military. The US Forces' role in conducting presence operations abroad is described in the DSG under the Provide a Stabilizing Presence mission as requiring "thoughtful choices regarding the location and frequency of these operations".[48] The Arctic may or may not be an area in which the military will increase under this guidance.

The US Navy considers the Arctic as a potential operating area. The 2007 Cooperative Strategy for 21St Century Seapower describes the Arctic as a region of "new resource development and new shipping routes that may reshape the global transport system"[49] A US Navy Arctic Roadmap was published in 2009 to identify the Navy's strategic objectives in the Arctic region, identify the activities to achieve those objectives and describe the investments necessary to develop capabilities in the Arctic.[50]

Under the direction of the Arctic Roadmap, the Navy published its strategic objectives for the Arctic region. The Navy's desired end state in the Arctic is a "safe, stable, secure Arctic region where US national and maritime interests are safeguarded, and the homeland is protected".[51] Under the roadmap, the immediate needs of the Arctic region are icebreaking vessels, search and rescue capabilities, and maritime law enforcement and safety monitoring. The Navy assesses that the US Coast Guard is capable of meeting these needs for the immediate future.

The Navy's Arctic roadmap and the Arctic Strategic Objectives undergo a review and update following each Quadrennial Defense Review (QDR). The upcoming 2014 QDR should generate changes in the Navy's Arctic planning considering the DSG directed rebalancing to the Pacific. The Arctic may decrease in priority when balanced against other regions of the world. Even if the Navy sees the Arctic as less of a priority, the changes in the Arctic ice coverage are occurring and the region will rise in prominence. The Marine Corps can leverage the Navy's Arctic planning to begin its own studies of the Arctic to determine when Arctic requirements may begin to increase.

The Marine Corps' major strategic documents do not address the Arctic as a specific or separated region in which to operate. Marine Corps Vision and Strategy 2025, which informs combatant commanders and the civilian leadership of the Marine Corps' contributions to national security, describes five global regions the Marine Corps will prioritize for operations. These are the littoral regions of East and Southeast Asia, the Middle East, Africa, Latin America and the Caribbean and the Mediterranean Sea.[52] The document does highlight the Marine Corps' expeditionary preparedness to operate in austere and inhospitable conditions and the Corps' institutional adaptability, both of which are traits that would be required in the Arctic.[53]

The upcoming QDR in 2014 and the subsequent review of the Navy Arctic Roadmap and Arctic Strategic Objectives will likely affect DoD thinking on the Arctic. It is conjecture to predict if the QDR will emphasize or de-emphasize the Arctic, but if the 2012 DSG is an indicator than it is possible the Arctic may not be a region of concern or significance. The QDR focuses on a four-year window and significant change in the Arctic and the economic viability of resource extraction will not likely occur before the next QDR in 2018. What is more certain is the environmental indications that the Arctic will continue to change over the long-term, generating global shifts in shipping and trade and energy resources, and will require the DoD to focus more on the area.

The Marine Corps' Way Ahead in the Arctic

The Arctic is not an immediate concern for Marine Corps operational planning, at least not up to 2025 as described in current Headquarters Marine Corps long range planning.[54] The current Arctic represents a similar time to the 1920's Pacific in Marine Corps thinking and concept development. At that time, major conflict in the Pacific was two decades away but planning for operations began among Marine Corps senior leadership. Concepts were tested, new equipment was developed, and new doctrine was created to solve the problem of landing forces on defended islands. During this period of concentration on the Pacific, combat operations were ongoing in Nicaragua and China.[55] Combat on the Pacific islands was conceptual, but this work led to the successful campaigns of WWII.

The Marine Corps faces a similar period of time, in the first third of the 21st century, to study the Arctic and develop concepts and plans. It is necessary to study the Arctic as a concept for the future while current strategic shifts, the focus on the Pacific for example, are ongoing.

The Arctic is not a foreign environment to the Marine Corps, and current operations in that region provide opportunities to study the complexities of MAGTF Arctic operations and build on existing capabilities.

The Marine Corps currently pre-positions equipment above the Arctic Circle in Norway. This equipment set supports a MAGTF built around an infantry battalion task force and a composite aviation squadron.[56] Marine Corps forces, usually drawn from the reserves, conduct exercises with other NATO forces in Norway, utilizing this equipment and developing skills for operating in the Arctic.[57] Maintaining this presence and equipment in the Arctic region provides a test bed for expanding the capabilities to operate in that region and adapt to the future potential changes.

The capability to operate in the Arctic, both for the Marine Corps and the other Naval Services, will be built around mission sets. The joint Marine Corps, Navy, and Coast Guard Cooperative Strategy for 21st Century Seapower describes the six broad capabilities that the Naval Services will perform: forward presence, deterrence, sea control, power projection, maritime security, and humanitarian assistance and disaster response.[58] The Arctic littorals are no exception to this strategy and the Naval Services can expect to conduct missions within all of these broad capability areas.

Operations in the Arctic littorals may be a novel expression of the Single Naval Battle Concept. The Single Naval Battle approach integrates the elements of the naval force into a cohesive whole. Marine Corps and Navy forces provide a multi-domain approach that eliminates the seams between air, land, and sea.[59] The operational limitations of the Arctic, namely ice-capable ships and command and control capability gaps, create a need for the elements of the Naval Services to complement each other in non-traditional ways. Land forces may provide sea control. Surface forces may provide navigation aids. These complementary capabilities are understood better when framed by the capability areas from the Cooperative Strategy for 21st Century Seapower.

Seapower operations in the Arctic will be inherently a forward presence operation. The distances involved in reaching the Arctic Ocean and the lack of infrastructure, particularly in the US Arctic and the NWP, will require forward deployed maritime assets. The US Coast Guard routinely establishes temporary forward basing areas in and above the Bering Strait in Alaska during the ice-free summer months to increase its capability to respond to incidents in the US Arctic waters.[60] The Marine Corps could similarly deploy to forward bases in the Arctic, potentially into areas where sea-ice prevents Navy and Coast Guard non-ice strengthened ships to operate.

Deterrence operations in the Arctic are not new to the Joint Force. US Strategic Command and NORAD conduct nuclear deterrence operations and homeland defense operations over and under the Arctic Ocean since the 1950's.[61] The nature of deterrence operations will change as the Arctic environment changes. Conventional deterrence operations will become as important as nuclear deterrence. Nations with icebreaker capabilities may be able to operate in Arctic waters that Navy and Coast Guard ships will not be able to reach. Ground, air and submarine forces will be the only conventional deterrent to incursions into US Arctic waters until ice-capable ships are brought on-line.

Sea control operations will face a similar challenge as deterrence operations. Controlling the sea in an icy region without ice-capable surface ships will become a ground, air and submarine mission. A possible solution to the sea control problem in the Arctic would be joint submarine and ground force operations to established localized sea, air and land dominance.

Land and air delivered fires may require navigation aids to augment GPS systems, surface ships outside of the ice zones may provide position and timing data to guided weapons.

Power projection operations will be important in the Arctic littorals. Ensuring freedom of passage in the NWP and the NSR will become a mission for the Naval Services. Partnering with allied nations like the Arctic NATO partners and other nations orienting towards the Arctic may help fill capability gaps in the US Naval Forces. Marine Corps forces partner with British, Norwegian and Dutch ships to land amphibious forces above the Arctic Circle in Norway during the Cold Response exercises.[62] Partnering may provide a solution to fill US and allied nation Arctic security problems.

Maritime security operations are the mission set the Coast Guard currently provides, on a limited scale, in the Arctic. Coast Guard assets in the Arctic conduct search and rescue, marine environmental protection, fisheries enforcement, marine safety and waterways management missions.[63] A future ice-free Arctic will likely require maritime security operations beyond the Coast Guard capability. The Marine Corps may find space in the maritime security operations area by augmenting the Coast Guard or operating off of Coast Guard ships. Collaborating with the Coast Guard now can give the Marine Corps access to the US Arctic and give Marine Corps planners an opportunity to gain an understanding of the Arctic outside of Norway.

Humanitarian assistance and disaster response operations are likely to increase in frequency as the human activity in the Arctic increases. Joint forces could be requested to respond to oil spills, shipping accidents or other man-made events. An example of this type of operation is the military assistance given to the Kulluk Salvage, a Royal Dutch Shell oil company mobile drilling barge that was grounded in a storm near Prudhoe Bay, Alaska in early 2013. During the response to the incident, Alaska Air National Guard helicopters staged out of a

US Coast Guard base to ferry supplies and repair parts to the barge.[64] Marine Corps forces could similarly work with Alaska National Guard and other state assets, Coast Guard forces and other interagency assets when operating in the Arctic.

Focusing closer on the sea control mission, the former Soviet Union provides a good study of the use of amphibious forces to address the challenges of military operations in the Arctic. In the mid-1980's the Center for Naval Analysis determined that in a conventional (non-nuclear) war with the US the Soviet Union would consider the Arctic as a vital strategic link between the North Atlantic and the North Pacific. To gain control of the Arctic region, the Soviet Armed Forces would seize the straits that make up the approaches to the Arctic Ocean, the Bering Strait, the passages through the Canadian Archipelago and Greenland and Norway.

The Soviets planned to use a joint amphibious campaign to seize and hold the straits. Naval forces would land ground troops supported by land-based aircraft. Using air and land forces and naval mines to hold and blockade the Arctic approaches would assure access to the Arctic for the Soviet Navy. Command of these approaches and the airspace above the Arctic would set the conditions for the Soviet Navy to establish control of the Arctic Ocean and deny its use to the US and NATO navies.[65] Marine Corps forces could operate in the Arctic in a mission set similar to the Soviets'.

It is possible that the US may have to project power or conduct sea control operations in the Arctic before sufficient ice-capable surface combatants come into service for the Navy, or before the ice conditions diminish to a level safe enough for non-ice capable ships. In a short duration conflict with limited naval forces opposing each other, submarine and air forces could suffice to establish sea control. A larger conflict involving peer competitors that takes place in the Atlantic or Pacific Oceans could create a situation where the US would require assured access to the Arctic sea lines of communication (SLOCs), the NWP and the NSR, while denying the region to hostile forces.

The attractiveness of the Arctic sea-lanes as a shorter route between Asia and eastern United States makes this scenario plausible. A potential US adversary may recognize the strategic value of the Arctic Straits to the US and seek to deny the Arctic passages and the distance advantages they provide. Rather than commit valuable naval and air forces to a fight on the periphery of the main theater, a MAGTF could achieve sea control in the narrows and straits that dominate the Arctic passages. This potential mission space is one Single Naval Battle concept the Marine Corps could pursue in the Arctic.

Employing a MAGTF in the Arctic to control the sea would not be the first use of Marine Corps forces to secure SLOCs. During WWII, the Marine Corps Defense Battalions secured islands throughout the South Pacific to maintain the SLOCs between the US and Australia.[66] The Defense Battalions were combined arms organizations made up of coastal defense artillery, anti-aircraft guns and a machine gun battery. Infantry companies were added to the battalions after the Battle of Wake Island.[67] The Defense Battalions were also equipped with the sensor systems of that era: radar, searchlights, radio direction-finding equipment and sound location systems.[68]

The original concept of operations for the Defense Battalions tasked them with defending strategically important Pacific islands. That concept was modified after the attack on Pearl Harbor to include offensive operations. By 1942 the Defense Battalions were conducting amphibious landings in the Samoan Island Chain. The mission of the Defense Battalions were to establish and defend airfields to support US Army Air Corps and Marine Corps aircraft, deny those islands to the Japanese, and free up naval surface combatants for offensive operations.[69]

By combining coastal artillery, anti-aircraft weapons, ground weapons, and sensors the Marine Corps created a unique capability that was adapted to support amphibious maneuver and to establish persistent sea-control.

An Arctic MAGTF could operate in a similar manner to the Defense Battalions to achieve the regional control similar to what the Soviets planned by establishing localized air, land and sea surface dominance on the SLOCs. Working with a submarine force, the MAGTF could establish full sea control. Adding a submarine to a MAGTF would not be easy; there are considerable command and control and technology issues to resolve. Unmanned underwater vehicles, perhaps armed, are another possible solution to extend the MAGTF capability beneath the surface of the sea.

Conceivably, a Special Purpose MAGTF organized like a Defense Battalion, built around a surface launched anti-ship missile system and an air-defense system, could provide a combined arms sea control capability in a narrow waterway like the Bering Strait. Fixed and Rotary wing air assets could extend the sensor range, targeting capability and strike capability of the MAGTF. Ground based air defense systems could provide local protection to the ground forces.

The Arctic oriented MAGTF described above could extend the range of non ice-capable naval forces into the ice zones and deny the approaches the Arctic Ocean to hostile ice capable forces. This type of operation could be an economy of force mission, controlling the sea from the land while the bulk of the Naval forces operate in other theaters or areas of the world. Adding partner nations to the operation would possibly increase the MAGTF capability and reduce the burden on US Naval forces.

Developing and testing this sea control concept and other concepts is possible in the current budget constrained environment. The NATO Arctic allies-Canada, Norway, and

Denmark-present opportunities for the Marine Corps to gain more experience in the Arctic and test the validity of operational concepts without adding additional budget pressure. Participating in the Arctic exercises in Norway and conducting security cooperation missions with Arctic countries may provide a low-cost solution to monitoring the state of the Arctic and generating concepts. Maintaining a degree of liaison with those countries will ensure a cadre of Arctic minded officers to remain engaged and focused on this area.

Close cooperation with less traditional joint and interagency partners is another potential avenue for the Marine Corps to gain an understanding of the Arctic. The US Coast Guard operates in the Arctic and maintains the only ice-capable ships in the US inventory. The Navy research and development community and the National Science Foundation conduct submarine borne scientific expeditions to study Arctic ice and environmental conditions. Leveraging these communities, the Marine Corps could access areas of the Arctic outside of Norway.

Challenges to Marine Corps and Joint Force Operations in the Arctic

The US military currently operates in the Arctic; however, there are technical limitations and capability gaps that challenge the ability of the Joint Force to conduct the full range of military operations. It is noted by the DoD that current capabilities are sufficient for the Arctic mission requirements right now, but these capability sets must be re-assessed as conditions in the Arctic change and human activity in the region increases.[70] Monitoring the status of these limitations and gaps, and shaping the solutions where appropriate, will inform the Marine Corps capability developers on when increased Arctic operations may be required.

The Navy and the US Coast Guard currently lack icebreaking and ice-capable ships. The Coast Guard maintains two icebreakers in its fleet: a heavy icebreaker capable of operating year-round in the Arctic and a medium icebreaker capable of operating in the lighter ice conditions of the spring, summer and fall.[71] This current icebreaking capability is deemed insufficient for the current Coast Guard mission requirements in the Arctic and not capable of supporting US Navy operations in the Arctic.[72] The Department of Homeland Security (DHS) is reviewing the budget options to fund additional Coast Guard icebreaker acquisitions in the future.

The US Navy does not maintain ice-capable surface combatant ships for employment in ice conditions. An ice-capable ship does not break ice, but is constructed with a reinforced hull that can withstand light ice conditions and ice impacts. Although the ice-coverage in the Arctic is shrinking and freeing up shipping routes, icebergs and light surface ice can always be present. Any ship operating in the region should be reinforced for safety.

Although surface combatants are limited in the Arctic, Navy submarines have operated in the region since 1958 and the submarine forces test and validate Arctic tactics and operations in periodic exercises.[73] The Navy is assessing its mission requirements for ice-capable surface ships in the Arctic for future budget submissions and maintains the US Navy Arctic Roadmap to monitor and track capability gaps and solutions.[74]

Communications and precision navigation in the Arctic is also a challenge to operations. US military navigation and communications systems are optimized for non-Arctic regions, degradation of these systems affect the safety and performance of military systems above the Arctic Circle.[75] The Global Positioning System (GPS) is less capable in the Arctic, with vertical navigation errors that affect precision-guided munitions due to the geometry of the satellite constellation in relation to GPS receivers and interference from the ionosphere.[76] Magnetic and inertial navigation devices become less precise in relation to the North Pole due to reduced effects of the Earth's rotation.[77] High Frequency and Very High Frequency communications experience increased disturbances and disruptions due to ionosphere effects that decrease the range and reliability of these systems.[78] Current communications and navigation capabilities in the Arctic are insufficient to support large-scale Joint Force operations.[79]

Conclusion

The Arctic is not the region the Marine Corps must plan for now, but it is a region the Marine Corps must plan for in the years beyond 2025. As human activity grows in the Arctic, the need for security will grow as well. Current capability gaps in ice-capable ships may persist into the future. The MAGTF may fill a gap in the Naval Services' ability to establish sea control in the Arctic by operating in the straits and narrow waterways that make up the NWP and NSR.

New concepts for amphibious operations and novel uses of the MAGTF may grow from planning for Arctic operations. The Soviet plans to establish sea and air control in the Arctic straits and the use of the Marine Corps Defense Battalions in WWII present a point of departure to shape Marine Corps concept development. These concepts, in turn, may drive the development of capabilities with application in other littoral areas and straits.

Thinking about the Arctic by considering the complexities of the environment and how a future Marine Corps may operate in the region presents an opportunity to develop concepts and test them at the edge of current MAGTF and Joint Force capability. Studying the Arctic in the first third of the 21st century ensures the Marine Corps readiness in the mid-century for an uncertain future in a strategically important region.

Endnotes

[1] "Arctic Sea Ice News & Analysis", National Snow and Ice Data Center Website, updated 2 March 2013, accessed 4 March 2013, http://nsidc.org/arcticseaicenews/.

[2] US President, National Security Policy Directive 66/Homeland Security Policy Directive 25, "Arctic Region Policy," (Washington, DC: January 1999) 3.

[3] "Arctic Climatology and Meteorology: What is the Arctic?," United States National Snow and Ice Data Center, accessed 14 January 2013, http://www.nsidc.org/basics/arctic_definition.html

[4] Committee on National Security Implications of Climate Change for US Naval Forces and National Research Council. *National Security Implications of Climate Change for US Naval Forces.* (Washington, DC: National Academies Press, 2011), 91 and Kříž, Zdeněk and Filip Chrášťanský. "Existing Conflicts in the Arctic and the Risk of Escalation: Rhetoric and Reality." *Perspectives: Central European Review of International Affairs* 20, no. 1 (07, 2012): 131.

[5] "Arctic Sea Ice News & Analysis", National Snow and Ice Data Center Website, updated 2 March 2013, accessed 4 March 2013, http://nsidc.org/arcticseaicenews/.

[6] Muyin Want and James E. Overstreet, "A Sea Ice Free Summer Arctic Within 30 Years?," *Geophysical Research Letters* 36, no. 1, 1-5.

[7] Figure 1: "Arctic Maps", National Snow and Ice Data Center Website, updated 2 March 2013, accessed 18 February 2013. http://nsidc.org/arcticmet/arctic_map .html.

[8] International Hydrography Organization

[9] "The Arctic Ocean", CIA World Factbook Website, updated 15 November 2012, accessed 4 March 2013. https://www.cia.gov/library/publications/the-world-factbook/geos/xq.html

[10] Donat Pharand, "The Arctic Waters and the Northwest Passage: A Final Revisit", *Ocean Development and International Law* 38, no. 3, 69.

[11] "The Canadian Maritime Arctic and Northwest Passage", ARCTIS Database Website, Centre for High North Logistics, updated 22 January 2013, accessed 4 March 2013. http://www.arctis-search.com/The+Canadian+Maritime+Arctic+and+Northwest+Passage&structure=Arctic+Sea+Routes.

[12] Douglas Brubaker, Russian Arctic Straits, (Leiden, NLD: Martinus Niijhoff Publishers, 2004, 6.

[13] Brubaker, 7-14.

[14] Titely and St. John. 39.

[15] "Arctic Shipping Routes – Cost Comparisons with Suez", ARCTIS Database Website, Centre for High North Logistics, updated 22 January 2013, accessed 4 March 2013. http://www.arctis-search.com/Arctic+Shipping+Routes+-+Cost+Comparisons+with+Suez&structure=Arctic+Sea+Routes.

[16] "NSR Transits 2012", ARCTIS Database Website, Centre for High North Logistics, updated 22 January 2013, accessed 4 March 2013. http://www.arctis-search.com/NSR+Transits+2012&structure=Arctic+Sea+Routes

[17] "Statistics on Transit Voyages", ARCTIS Database Website, Centre for High North Logistics, updated 22 January 2013, accessed 4 March 2013. http://www.arctis-search.com/Statistics+on+Transit+Voyages&structure=Arctic+Sea+Routes.

[18] Michael Byers, "Canada's Not Ready to Have the World in the Arctic", *Globe and Mail*, 15 August 2012.

[19] US Geological Survey, 1. and Titely and St. John, 38.

[20] US Geological Survey, 1.

[21] US Geological Survey 1. and Philip Budzek, "Arctic Oil and Natural Gas Potential," (Washington D.C: US Energy Information Administration, October 2009), 4.

[22] Budzek, 5. The EEZ is defined by the UNCLOS as the 200 NM extension of national territory in the ocean.

[23] "Total Energy", US Energy Information Administration Website, updated 27 September 2012. Accessed 4 March 2013. http://www.eia.gov/totalenergy/data /annual /showtext.cfm?t=ptb0402.

[24] Budzek, 7.

[25] Yury Morozov, "Arctic 2030: What are the Consequences of Climate Change?: The Russian Response," *Bulletin of the Atomic Scientists* 68, no. 4, 25. and Budzek, 5.

[26] Budzek, 9.

[27] Bureau of Land Management, 7. and Titely and St. John, 39.

[28] Heather Conley and Jamie Kraut, US Strategic Interests in the Arctic: An Assessment of Current Challenges and New Opportunities for Cooperation, (Washington, D.C.: Center for Strategic and International Studies, 2010), 4.

[29] Dmitry Bogoyavlenskiy, Andy Siggner, Arctic Human Development Report: Arctic Demography, Arctic Human Development Report 2004, Akureyri: Stefansson Arctic Institute. http://www.svs.is/ahdr/AHDR%20chapters/ English% 20version/ AHDR_chp%202.pdf. Accessed Jan 30 2013.

[30] Dmitry Bogoyavlenskiy, Andy Siggner, Arctic Human Development Report: Arctic Demography, Arctic Human Development Report 2004, Akureyri: Stefansson Arctic Institute. http://www.svs.is/ahdr/AHDR%20chapters/ English% 20version/ AHDR_chp%202.pdf. Accessed Jan 30 2013.

[31] City of Barrow website: http://www.cityofbarrow.org/content/view/5/5/. Accessed Jan 30 2013.

[32] Arctic 2030 Consequences of Climate Change: Russia, 23.

[33] NSPD-66/HSPD-25 3.

[34] NSPD-66/HSPD-25 4.

[35] Defense R&D Canada, Centre for Operational Research and Analysis, "Arctic Planning Scenarios: Scenario #1: Defense Scenario", (Ottowa, ON: Canada Defense, July 2011), 13.

[36] Zdeněk Kříž and Filip Chráštanský, "Existing Conflicts in the Arctic and the Risk of Escalation: Rhetoric and Reality," *Perspectives Central European Review of International Affairs* 20, no. 1, 2012, 131.

[37] Malte Humpert and Andreas Raspotnik, "The Future of Arctic Shipping," Port Technology 55, October 2012, 11.

[38] William.G.Huff, *The Economic Growth of Singapore*, (Cambridge: Cambridge University Press, 1994), 8.

[39] Huff, 120.

[40] Huff, 8-10, 17.

[41] "The world Factbook Singapore", CIA Website, accessed 30 Jan 2013 https://www.cia.gov/library/publications/the-world-factbook/geos/sn.html. and 'Top 50 World Container Ports" The World Shipping Council website, accessed 30 Jan 2013 http://www.worldshipping.org/about-the-industry/global-trade/top-50-world-container-ports.

[42] Carolyn Cartier. Cosmopolitics and the Maritime World City, *Geographical Review*, Vol 89, No. 2, Apr 1999, 280 - 281. http://www.jstor.org/stable/216092.

[43] Cartier, 281.

[44] "San Francisco", City Data Website, accessed 30 January 2013, http://www.city-data.com/us-cities/The-West/San-Francisco-Economy.html.

[45] US President, "National Security Strategy," (Washington, DC: May 2010), 50.

[46] Secretary of Defense, "2010 Quadrennial Defense Review," (Washington, DC: Office of the Secretary of Defense, 12 February 2010) 42, 80, 82, 85, 109

[47] Chairman of the Joint Chiefs of Staff, "National Military Strategy of the United States," (Washington, DC.: Joint Chiefs of Staff, 8 February 2011) 11.

[48] US President, "Sustaining US Global Leadership: Priorities for the 21st Century Defense," (Washington, DC., 3 January 2012) 5.

[49] Commandant of the Marine Corps, Chief of Naval Operations and Commandant of the Coast Guard, "A Cooperative Strategy for 21st Century Seapower," (Washington, DC.: Government Printing Office, October 2007), 6.

[50] Chief of Naval Operations, "USN Arctic Roadmap" (Washington, DC: Navy Task Force Climate Change, October 2009), 9.

[51] Chief of Naval Operations, "US Navy Arctic Strategic Objectives," (Washington, DC.: Navy Task for Climate Change, 21 May 2010), 2.

[52] Commandant of the Marine Corps, "Marine Corps Vision and Strategy 2025" (Washington, DC.: Headquarters Marine Corps, 15 August 2010), 25.

[53] Marine Corps Vision and Strategy 2025, 6.

[54] Marine Corps Vision and Strategy 2025.

[55] J. Robert Moskin, *The US Marine Corps Story*, (New York: Little, Brown and Company, 1992) 219-224.

[56] Marine Corps Forces Europe Press Release, MFE/Norway cross-leveling operation marks shift in Marine Corps pre-positioning posture, June 29, 2012.

[57] Marine Corps Times, Norway Exercise Preps Marines for Cold Combat, March 24, 2012.

[58] A Cooperative Strategy for 21st Century Seapower, 14.

[59] Headquarters, US Marine Corps, *Naval Amphibious Capability in the 21st Century: Strategic Opportunity and a Vision for Change*, Report of the Amphibious Capabilities Working Group (Washington, D.C.: Headquarters Marine Corps, 27 April 2012), 33.

[60] US Government Accountability Office, *Coast Guard Observations on Arctic Requirements, Icebreakers, and Coordination with Stakeholders*, GAO Report GAO-12-254T (Washington D.C.: Government Accountability Office, 1 December 2011) 6, 21.

[61] US Navy Arctic Roadmap, 6.

[62] Commanding Officer, 24th Marine Regiment, "After Action Report For Exercise Cold Response 28 Feb – 24 Mar 2012.", to Commanding General 4th Marine Division, 30 April 2012, 7-11.

[63] US Navy Arctic Strategic Objectives, 2.

[64] SSgt Barnett, Robert, "Army Helicopters Aid Stranded Oil Rig," Air Force Times, 9 January 2013.

[65] Charles C. Petersen, *Soviet Military Objectives in the Arctic Theater and How They Might be Attained*, (Alexandria, VA: Center for Naval Analysis, 10 November 1986), 4, 7, 8.

[66] Steven Maynard, "Marine Defense Battalions, October 1939-December 1942: Their Contributions in the Early Phases of World War II," Masters thesis, University of North Texas, 1996, 148-149.

[67] Charles Updegraph, *US Marine Corps Special Units of World War II*, (Washington, D.C.: Historical Division, Headquarters, US Marine Corps, 1972). 72-75.

[68] Updegraph, 62. and Maynard, 17, 21.

[69] Maynard, 148-149.

[70] Undersecretary of Defense (Policy), "A Report to Congress on Arctic Operations and the Northwest Passage," (Washington, D.C.: Department of Defense, May 2011), 15.

[71] GAO report, Coast Guard Testimony on the Arctic 2011, p 10.

[72] Ibid, p 13.

[73] A Report to Congress on Arctic Operations and the Northwest Passage, 17.

[74] US Navy Arctic Roadmap. 9.

[75] Committee on National Security Implications of Climate Change for US Naval Forces and National Research Council. *National Security Implications of Climate Change for US Naval Forces*, (Washington, D.C: National Academies Press, 2011), 106

[76] Committee on National Security Implications of Climate Change for US Naval Forces 113.

[77] Committee on National Security Implications of Climate Change for US Naval Forces 113.

[78] Committee on National Security Implications of Climate Change for US Naval Forces 101.

[79] A Report to Congress on Arctic Operations and the Northwest Passage, 16.

Bibliography

Primary Sources

Chairman of the Joint Chiefs of Staff, "National Military Strategy of the United States," Washington, DC: Joint Chiefs of Staff, 8 February 2011.

Chairman, National Intelligence Council, *Global Trends 2030: Alternative Worlds*, Washington, DC: National Intelligence Council, December 2012, accessed 04 February 2013, Http://www.dni.gov/nic/globaltrends.

Chief of Naval Operations, "US Navy Arctic Roadmap," Washington, DC: Navy Task Force Climate Change, October 2009.

Chief of Naval Operations, "US Navy Arctic Strategic Objectives," Washington, DC: Navy Task for Climate Change, 21 May 2010.

Commandant of the Marine Corps, "Marine Corps Vision and Strategy 2025," Washington, DC: Headquarters Marine Corps, 15 August 2010.

Commandant of the Marine Corps, Chief of Naval Operations and Commandant of the Coast Guard, "A Cooperative Strategy for 21st Century Seapower," Washington, DC: Government Printing Office, October 2007.

Commanding Officer, 24th Marine Regiment, "After Action Report For Exercise Cold Response 28 Feb – 24 Mar 2012." To Commanding General 4th Marine Division, 30 April 2012.

Defense R&D Canada, Centre for Operational Research and Analysis, "Arctic Planning Scenarios: Scenario #1: Defense Scenario", Ottawa, ON: Canada Defense, July 2011.

Headquarters, US Marine Corps, *Naval Amphibious Capability in the 21st Century: Strategic Opportunity and a Vision for Change*, Report of the Amphibious Capabilities Working Group, Washington, DC: Headquarters Marine Corps, 27 April 2012.

Undersecretary of Defense (Policy), "A Report to Congress on Arctic Operations and the Northwest Passage," Washington, DC: Department of Defense, May 2011.

Secretary of Defense, "2010 Quadrennial Defense Review," Washington, DC: Office of the Secretary of Defense, 12 February 2010.

Updegraph, Charles L., *US Marine Corps Special Units of World War II*, Washington, DC: Historical Division, Headquarters, US Marine Corps, 1972.

US Department of the Interior, Bureau of Land Management, "Mineral Resources of Western Arctic Alaska", Anchorage, AK: Bureau of Land Management, 1991.

US Government Accountability Office, *Arctic Capabilities: DOD Addressed Many Specified Reporting Elements in its 2011 Arctic Report but should Take Steps to Meet Near and Long-Term Needs*, Washington, DC: US Government Accountability Office, Jan 2012.

US Government Accountability Office, *Coast Guard Observations on Arctic Requirements, Icebreakers, and Coordination with Stakeholders*, GAO Report GAO-12-254T, Washington DC: Government Accountability Office, 1 December 2011

US Department of the Interior, US Geological Survey, "Circum-Arctic Resource Appraisal: Estimates of Undiscovered Oil and Gas North of the Arctic Circle," Washington, DC: US Geological Survey, 2008.

US President, Directive, "Arctic Region Policy (NSPD-66/HSPD-25)," Washington, DC: January 2009.

US President, "National Security Strategy," Washington, DC: May 2010.

US President, "Sustaining US Global Leadership: Priorities for the 21st Century Defense," Washington, DC, 3 January 2012.

Secondary Sources

Bogoyavlenskiy, Dimitry and Andy Siggner, "Arctic Human Development Report 2004: Arctic Demography", (Akureyri: Stefansson Arctic Institute. August 2004) Accessed 30 January, 2013. http://www.svs.is/ahdr/AHDR%20chapters/ English% 20version/ AHDR_chp%202.pdf.

Brubaker, Douglas, *Russian Arctic Straits*, Leiden, NLD: Martinus Nijhoff Publishers, December 2004.

Budzik, Philip. *Arctic Oil and Natural Gas Potential*. Washington, DC: US Energy Information Administration, 2009.

Cartier, Carolyn, "Cosmopolitics and the Maritime World City," *Geographical Review*, Vol 89, No. 2, Apr 1999, 280 - 281.

Chalecki, Elizabeth L., "He Who Would Rule: Climate Change in the Arctic and its Implications for US National Security," *Journal of Public and International Affairs* 18, Spring 2007, 204-222.

Conley, Heather and Jamie Kraut, *US Strategic Interests in the Arctic: An Assessment of Current Challenges and New Opportunities for Cooperation*, Washington, DC: Center for Strategic and International Studies, 2010.

Committee on National Security Implications of Climate Change for US Naval Forces, *National Security Implications of Climate Change for US Naval Forces*, (Washington, DC: National Academies Press, 2011.

Emmerson, Charles and Glada Lahn, "Arctic Opening: Opportunity and Risk in the High North," London: Lloyd's and Chatham House, 2012.

Huff, William G, *The Economic Growth of Singapore*, Cambridge: Cambridge University Press, 1994.

Humpert, Malte and Raspotnik, Andreas, "The Future of Arctic Shipping," *Port Technology* 55, October, 2012.

Johnston, Peter F., *Arctic Energy Resources and Global Energy Security,* Journal of Military and Strategic Studies 12, no. 2, Winter 2010.

Kříž, Zdeněk and Filip Chrášťanský. "Existing Conflicts in the Arctic and the Risk of Escalation: Rhetoric and Reality," *Perspectives: Central European Review of International Affairs* 20, no 1, 111-139.

Maynard, Stephen R. "Marine Defense Battalion, October 1939-December 1942: Their Contributions in the Early Phases of World War II," Masters thesis, University of North Texas, 1996.

Moskin, Robert J., *The US Marine Corps Story*, New York: Little, Brown and Company, 1992.

Morozov, Yury "Arctic 2030: What are the Consequences of Climate Change?: The Russian Response," *Bulletin of the Atomic Scientists* 68, no. 4, 21-30.

Murray, Robert W. "Arctic Politics and the Emerging Multipolar System: Challenges and Consequences," *The Polar Journal* 2, no. 1, Jun 2012, 7-20.

Petersen, Charles C., *Soviet Military Objectives in the Arctic Theater and How They Might be Attained*, Alexandria, VA: Center for Naval Analysis, 10 November 1986.

Pharand, Donat, "The Arctic Waters and the Northwest Passage: A Final Revist," *Ocean Development and International Law* 38, no. 3, 3-69.

Russell, Denise, *Who Rules the Waves?: Piracy, Overfishing, and Mining the Ocean.* London, GBR: Pluto Press, 2010.

Titely, David W., and Courtney C. St. John, "Arctic Security Considerations and the US Navy's Roadmap for the Arctic," *Naval War College Review* 63, no. 2, Spring 2010, 35-42.

Wang, M. and J.E. Overland, "A Sea Ice Free Summer Arctic Within 30 Years?" *Geophysical Research Letters* 36, no. 7, April 2009.

Rampal, P., Weiss, J., Dubois, J.M., "IPCC Climate Models Do Not Capture Arctic Sea Ice Drift Acceleration: Consequences in Terms of Projected Sea Ice Thinning and Decline," *Journal of Geophysical Research* 116, no. C8, August 2011, 2156-2206.

Weeks, Stanley B., *Scanning the Horizon: Implications for Navy Strategy of National, Joint and Other Services' Strategic Trends,* Alexandria, VA: Center for Naval Analysis, February 2012.

Websites

Arctic Sea Ice News & Analysis", National Snow and Ice Data Center Website, updated 2 March 2013, accessed 4 March 2013, http://nsidc.org/arcticseaicenews.

"Arctic Shipping Routes – Cost Comparisons with Suez", ARCTIS Database Website, Centre for High North Logistics, updated 22 January 2013, accessed 4 March 2013. http://www.arctis-search.com/Arctic+Shipping+Routes+-+Cost+Comparisons+with+Suez&structure=Arctic+Sea+Routes.

"Arctic Council Observers", *Arctic Council* , accessed 22 February 2013, http://www.arctic-council.org/index.php/en/about-us/partners-links.

"Arctic Maps", National Snow and Ice Data Center Website, updated 2 March 2013, accessed 18 February 2013. http://nsidc.org/arcticmet/arctic_map .html.

City of Barrow Website, Accessed Jan 30 2013. http://www.cityofbarrow.org/content/view/5/5/.

"The world Factbook Singapore", CIA Website, accessed 30 Jan 2013 https://www.cia.gov/library/publications/the-world-factbook/geos/sn.html

"Statistics on Transit Voyages", ARCTIS Database Website, Centre for High North Logistics, updated 22 January 2013, accessed 4 March 2013. http://www.arctis-search.com/Statistics+on+Transit+Voyages&structure=Arctic+Sea+Routes.

"Arctic Shipping Routes – Cost Comparisons with Suez", ARCTIS Database Website, Centre for High North Logistics, updated 22 January 2013, accessed 4 March 2013. http://www.arctis-search.com/Arctic+Shipping+Routes+-+Cost+Comparisons+with+Suez&structure=Arctic+Sea+Routes.

"NSR Transits 2012", ARCTIS Database Website, Centre for High North Logistics, updated 22 January 2013, accessed 4 March 2013. http://www.arctis-search.com/NSR+Transits+2012&structure=Arctic+Sea+Routes

"Total Energy", US Energy Information Administration Website, updated 27 September 2012. Accessed 4 March 2013. http://www.eia.gov/totalenergy/data /annual /showtext.cfm?t=ptb0402.